LOVE

How Our family Was Made

(A Love Story for My Child)

How Our
Family
Was Made

(A Love Story for My Child)

ISBN: 979-8-218-04601-9 (Paperback)
ISBN: 979-8-218-04602-6 (Epub)

One particular family inspired the creation of this book with the hope of expanding kid lit and all publishing genres to include and respect and celebrate and support all kinds of healthy, loving families.

To my precious daughter whose many questions and comments inspired this book. I love you.

This book is also dedicated to you, reader, and to your family with appreciation for however it was made—by blood, by choice, by proximity, by allyship, by circumstance, by…

Once upon a time there was a
Beloved Little Girl who was smart, strong,
generous, kind, loving, and adventurous.
Going to interesting places, meeting
different people, reading books, and
learning facts and philosophies made her
very happy.

learning to
speak
SPANISH MANDARIN FRENCH GERMAN ARABIC
SWIMMING LESSONS
Annual
CAMP
adventure
fun
CIRCUS
Music
Lessons
gymnastics
SCHOOL
Ballet
Books
Theater Classes

As she grew into a Beloved Woman she made friends around her neighborhood, at school, at church, during her travels, while pursuing her hobbies, and at work.

HEALTHY & HAPPY FRIENDSHIP

All around her other people were finding their special someone to love and to marry, which made her happy to see. Their happiness encouraged her to believe her own happily-ever-after was getting closer to becoming a reality.

WEDDING
WEDDING PLANS
PHOTOS!
THE DRESSES!   THE DRAMA!
love
THE COUPLE
EXCHANGING
THEIR VOWS

In the meantime, Beloved Woman kept being smart, strong, generous, kind, loving, adventurous, resilient, and successful while she searched for her special someone.

HIGH SCHOOL
COLLEGE
BOOKS
Dating
feeling hopeful
community

She kept exploring
the world.

Arctic Ocean
NORTH AMERICAN BOREAL FORESTS
MOUNTAINS
INNER ASIA
Atlantic Ocean
SOUTH ASIA and BAY of BENGAL
GREATER MEKON
MESOAMERICA and WESTERN CARIBBEAN
SUDANO-SAHEL
ANDES, AMAZON, and ORINOCO
CENTRAL AFRICA and GULF of GUINEA
EASTERN AFRICA, MADAGASCAR, and WESTERN INDIAN OCEAN
SOU A
Indian Ocean
PATAGONIA
Pacific Ocean
THEAST ASIAN ARCHIPELAGO
MELANESIA
MONDAY
TUESDAY
WEDNESDAY
THURSDAY
FRIDAY
SATURDAY
SUNDAY
MONDAY
TUESDAY
WEDNESDAY
THURSDAY
FRIDAY
SATURDAY
SUNDAY
MONDAY
TUESDAY
WEDNESDAY
THURSDAY
FRIDAY
SATURDAY
SUNDAY

But she couldn't find them.

No matter how many introductions or romantic dates or destinations or events, she never crossed paths with her special someone when she felt ready to grow her own branch of her family tree.

N
W E
S
Building
Dreams
community

Beloved Woman considered her parenting options: become a foster parent, adopt a child, have a child through a surrogate or physically give birth to a child.

FOSTER
sandbox with canopy

After a lot of research, medical counseling, meditation, and prayer she chose to give birth because she wanted a close genetic connection with her child, and she wanted to experience being pregnant.

Fortunately, medical science and donations of reproductive material from many generous people for use by other people, like Beloved Woman, who haven't found their special someone by the time they're ready to have a baby made it possible for her to get pregnant.

She studied the information provided about donors before she picked the one who seemed just right.

Smart doctors used their scientific formula, like a recipe, to mix Beloved Woman's genetic reproductive material with the donor's, then they followed the steps that made Beloved Woman pregnant.

During her pregnancy Beloved Woman took good care of herself.

A Leap Of Faith
A Leap of Faith

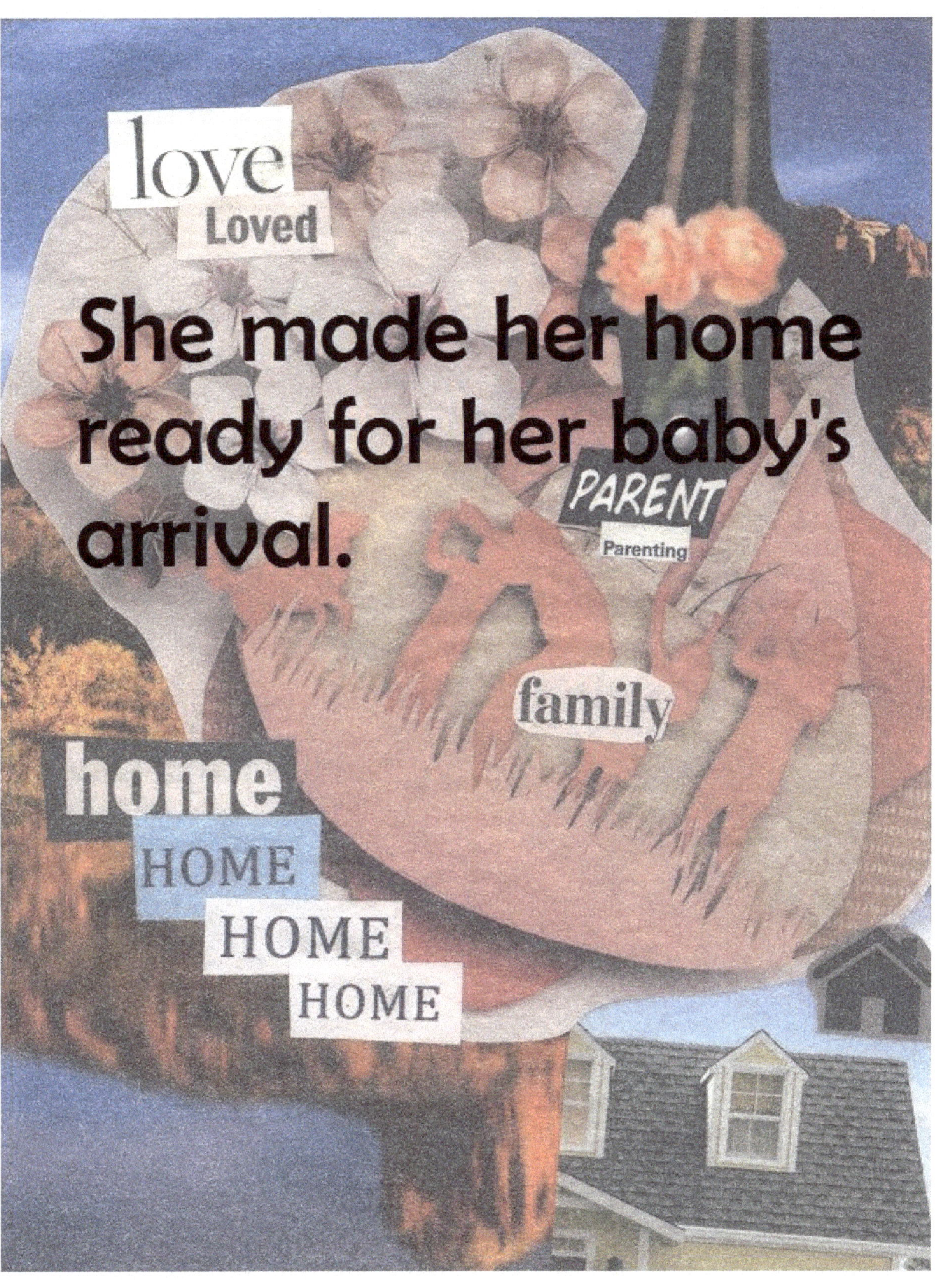

love
Loved
She made her home ready for her baby's arrival.
PARENT
Parenting
family
home
HOME
HOME
HOME

When her baby was born Beloved Woman looked into her child's face and recognized the special someone she was meant to love...

Making them a family of two as part of an extended family of parents, grandparents, aunties, uncles, siblings, cousins, steps, in-laws, fosters, friends, playmates, schoolmates, neighbors, human beings, and divine creations.

BWAH BUH
DAA

parent
child

Resources

Single Mothers By Choice

https://www.singlemothersbychoice.org/

Child Welfare Information Gateway

https://www.childwelfare.gov/nfcad/

About the Authors and Illustrators

Beloved Woman is an attorney.

The senior members of Banks Art Partners are retired educators and married college sweethearts.

The third member of BAP is their daughter.